BIBLICAL REVELATIONS
BY RAY MARION

RAY MARION

WESTBOW
PRESS
A DIVISION OF THOMAS NELSON
& ZONDERVAN

Nestle-Aland Greek English New Testament.

WestBow Press books may be ordered through booksellers or by contacting:

WestBow Press
A Division of Thomas Nelson & Zondervan
1663 Liberty Drive
Bloomington, IN 47403
www.westbowpress.com
1 (866) 928-1240

ISBN: 978-1-4908-5443-4 (sc)
ISBN: 978-1-4908-5442-7 (e)

Library of Congress Control Number: 2014917466

Printed in the United States of America.

WestBow Press rev. date: 10/03/2014

What is part of Mystery Babylon in the Book of Revelation? In the Babylonian religion, when a person died, their soul was weighed in a balance, if it was more good than bad, it got eternal life. The Pope and Cardinals and Roman Catholic clergy teach that if you're more good than bad, you get eternal life which is Babylon's message. Dr.Scott taught that the 7 churches in Revelation appear in sequence historically. Historically means you have to go outside the Bible to understand the prophecies. Dr.Scott taught on 5 of the 7 churches. All he said about Thyatira was that it was the church of the dark ages. Jezebel was the leader of the false church in the old testament. Jezebel in the Thyatira letter is a parable of the bishop of Rome. Thyatira started when the bishop of Rome took the title Pontificus Maximus from the last Caesar. Damascus, bishop of Rome took this title in 431 A.D. Jesus promised Thyatira death. The mother of harlots in Revelation is Mystery Babylon and is the false church and is the Roman Catholic Church. In Revelation, the city that rules over the kings of the earth is Vatican City headed by the bishop

Rome also known as the Pope. The Pontificus Maximus in the Roman Empire was the leader of the mystery religion of the Roman Empire.

Spending money is an act of worship. How the chosen are separated from those not chosen in the true church of Jesus Christ is that the chosen will pay tithes, firstfruits and offerings of money to their respective preacher. Christians that don't pay are no different than atheists and are cast into hell for free by Jesus The Christ. The place that where God is fair in the Bible, it didn't matter if you were rich or poor, the tithe went into the Lord's storehouse which is to the preacher of the word. I believe where Jesus won't be fair, is at the judgment seat of Christ. In the parable of being granted authority over 5 cities and 10 cities, it's a parable, it will be like being given authority over 5 planets and 10 planets because we will conquer the new heaven and new earth.

Parts of the Tabernacle, Solomon's Temple and Ezekiel's Temple represented persons. For example, Paul said in Hebrews that the veil was Jesus' flesh which is his body which is his person. Later, John wrote in the Book of Revelation that the seven golden lampstands are the seven churches which word church in Greek I learned from Dr.Scott means out/called/ones which refers to persons. I learned from Dr. Scott that the golden boards of the Tabernacle represented the saints in Christ Jesus with the gold symbolizing the holy spirit in us and the wood symbolizing our human side. He taught as did scholars that the ark of the covenant symbolized the incarnation of Jesus Christ with the gold symbolizing the holy spirit and the acacia wood symbolizing his human side. I believe that the two corner boards represented that last two witnesses Elijah and Moses just like the two giant cherubims in the Holy of Holies of Solomon's temple symbolized Elijah and Moses. The two cherubims on the ark of the covenant symbolized Elijah and Moses. Two of the cherubims in Ezekiel's Temple will represent the last two witnesses Elijah and Moses. Chapter 11 of Revelation says that the last two witnesses are symbolized as lampstands. I believe that the lampstand in the Tabernacle symbolized John the revelator and that the ten golden lampstands in Solomon's temple symbolized the ten martyred apostles. The ten golden lampstands in Solomon's temple either represented the ten said apostles or ten churches. There's no way they represented ten churches, there was only one church during Solomon's reign. The veil represented 3 persons. Paul said the veil was Jesus' flesh which is his person. The veil also had the two cherubims which symbolized the last two witnesses Elijah and Moses. Aaron parted this veil one day a year on the day of atonement. When the veil was torn in two from top to bottom at Jesus' death, this symbolized that the day of atonement and the two cherubims would be cut and pasted and that it was cut and pasted to the second half of the feast of the trumpets which I learned from Dr. Scott is when the rapture takes place which is Revelation 4:1. Immediately after the rapture, this is when the identity of the antichrist will be revealed and the identities of the last two witnesses Elijah and Moses. Paul said Jesus was the substance of the set times which are the feast days. Paul was partly wrong. Jesus didn't fulfill Pentecost and won't fulfill the day of atonement feast. Elijah and Moses will fulfill the feast the day of atonement in a new way. Instead of Israelites afflicting their souls for one day on the day of atonement, the whole world during the first half of the great tribulation will be afflicted by the plagues of Elijah and Moses. This shall be the feast of atonement. Dr.Scott taught that the altar of burnt offering which had a purple cloth symbolized Jesus Christ as king. Dr.Scott taught that the altar of burnt offering typified calvary and that the four sides of the altar typified the world and its height of five cubits typified grace.

I believe the ten fine twined curtains in the Tabernacle represented the ten martyred apostles except John. I believe the eleven curtains made of goats' hair represented the eleven apostles. What did the goats hairs represent in these curtains? It represented an Israelite message. The message of the eleven was Jesus was raised from the dead and you have to keep the law, that was their message until Paul came on the scene with the new gospel. The curtain of rams skins dyed red symbolized Jesus Christ like Issac the miracle promised child. Abraham offered up a ram instead of his son Issac. Dr. Scott and Jack Zavada taught that the altar on incense typified the prayer life. The golden lampstand in the Tabernacle symbolized the church and the apostle John separately. Dr. Scott and scholars taught that the silver tenons with silver symbolizing redemption and the tenons literally means hands which is God's hands holding up the boards (the saints) upright and secured. Dr. Scott and scholars taught that the door of the Tabernacle symbolized the four gospels with its colours. Dr.Scott and scholars taught that the door of the Tabernacle symbolized the four gospels which spoke of Christ and that the purple symbolized Matthew's gospel that spoke of Jesus as King and that the white symbolized Luke's gospel with Jesus as the perfect man and that scarlet symbolized Mark's gospel as Jesus as the suffering servant and that blue symbolized John's gospel with blue as Jesus' eternal side. The cherubims woven into the veil symbolized Elijah and Moses, they were the two men in shining garments at the Ascension that preached to the disciples. The veil symbolized 3 persons, this was Elijah and Moses and they appeared at the Mount of Transfiguration speaking with Jesus. Dr.Scott also taught that the silver chain that ties the top of the Tabernacle symbolized redemption and lead to one door which spoke of Jesus Christ. He also taught that the word church in Greek is eklesia which means out/called/ones and refers to persons. Historically, he taught that it comes from a person walking down the street and calling people out of their houses. The calling would have a purpose.

The Tabernacle was first constructed in the 15th century B.C., About 1,500 years would go by before Paul revealed that the veil was Jesus' flesh and revealing that part of the Tabernacle represented a person. A few years later John wrote in the book of Revelation that the seven golden lampstands are the seven churches which refers to persons as part of the Tabernacle. About 2000 years would go by before Jesus Christ revealed through Dr.Scott more parts about the Tabernacle, finally, Jesus revealed through me parts of the Tabernacle, Solomon's Temple and Ezekiel's Temple. Finally, I believe that the middle golden bar of the Tabernacle symbolized Paul's ministry while the other 4 golden bars symbolized the 4 gospels. The middle golden bar which symbolized Paul's minitstry was at a height of 5 sacred cubits and I learned from Dr.Scott that 5 is the number of grace. The height of the burnt offering altar was at the same height of the middle golden bar and at a height of 5 sacred cubits was the number of grace.

I learned from Dr.Scott's teaching on the great pyramid that the pyramid inch is 1/500,000,000 division of the earth's axis and that 25 pyramid inches is the sacred cubit and that it's the measuring unit for Noah's Ark, The Tabernacle, Solomon's Temple and will be used for Ezekiel's Temple.

What about the table of showbread? Dr.Scott taught that the table of showbread wasn't a type of Jesus Christ. It was national giving that didn't have a redemptive value. During the feast of tabernacles, the nations that remain will give to the King of kings under penalty of plague and receive rain as a blessing for giving. I don't believe this giving will have a redemptive quality, it's a blessing of rain only. I believe worshipping Jesus Christ during the feast of tabernacles will be done by tares. God didn't redeem a nation at any time. I don't believe that if a nation worships the Kings of kings that they will be redeemed.

The veil of the Tabernacle symbolized Jesus, Elijah and Moses. I believe that the 3 men that met Abraham was the Lord, Michael and Gabriel with Michael symbolizing Elijah and Gabriel symbolizing Moses as a type of the last two witnesses. Abraham gave an offering of food to them. The two angels went and rescued Lot out of Sodom, he was a survivor. In the Book of Revelation, in chapter 11, Jerusalem is spiritually called Sodom and Egypt. Why is Jerusalem called Sodom? Lot fled Sodom to a place of refuge. I learned from Dr.Scott that Jews will flee Jerusalem (Sodom) to the geography of ancient Moab for a place of refuge. The two angels in Sodom symbolized the last two witnesses Elijah and Moses in spiritual Sodom which is Jerusalem. Why is Jerusalem spiritually called Egypt in Revelation? Ten plagues were poured out on ancient Egypt when Moses was in Egypt. The last two witnesses Elijah and Moses will pour out plagues globally from Jerusalem which is spiritual Egypt.

At the door of The Garden of Eden stood the Lord and two cherubims. It's the same picture as the veil of the Tabernacle symbolizing 3 persons. The two cherubims at the door of The

Garden of Eden symbolized Elijah and Moses. the last two witnesses.

Elijah and Moses show up on the stage of history sometimes together and sometimes separately. Dr.Scott claimed to be Elijah. I believe he was Elijah.

Passover was from the God of Jacob while the Day of Atonement was from the God of Israel. John said, "Behold the Lamb of God. He didn't say, " Behold the goat of God", which would indicate Jesus was the Day of Atonement goat. Jesus as the Passover Lamb had a redemptive quality while the Day of Atonement goat, its blood, could only forgive sins for 1 year and only for Israelites, it couldn't redeem persons like Rahab and Ruth.

In chapter 11 of the Book of Revelation Jerusalem is spiritually called Sodom. Lot fled for a place of refuge. The two angels in Sodom symbolized the last two witnesses Elijah and Moses. Dr.Scott taught from the Book of Daniel and said that the Jews will flee Jerusalem and flee to the ancient geography of Moab as a place of refuge from the face of the antichrist. I believe these Jews will still be under Satan's control. Peter wasn't too bright in saying that Lot was a righteous man. Lot was more righteous than the men of Sodom but I don't think he was a chosen vessel of God. In chapter 11 of Revelation Jerusalem is spiritually called Egypt. Ten plagues were poured out on ancient Egypt, the last two witnesses will have authority over all plagues globally. Dr.Scott taught that Egypt is a type of bondage to sin and a type of the world. The Jews will flee to Moab because the antichrist will set up the abomination of desolation spoken of by Daniel the prophet and Paul revealed that the antichrist will show himself as a god in the temple.

The Temple in the New Testament went through a transition. When Zacharias was a priest of the course of Abia the Temple was God's place of worship. When the widow put in her two mites it wasn't God's place of worship. Jesus wasn't teaching his disciples to put money into the Jewish treasury. The widow with the two mites is contrasted with the woman with the alabaster box, her offering was to Jesus and had an eternal value.

There are no accidents in the pyramid. The 7 tiers that open up the grand gallery means something. They represent the 7 churches in the Book of Revelation.

If I remember correctly, there's a small messianic triangle in the pyramid that represents Paul's ministry. I don't think that triangle includes his trip to Britain which has to do with the discovery of the 29th chapter of Acts in the year 1800 A.D. The messianic triangle has the dates 46 A.D. to 58 A.D.

There's something that Dr.Scott taught about Paul and I don't know which is right. In one teaching, he said Paul died of old age in Switzerland and in another teaching he said Paul was beheaded in Rome. I don't know what happened to Paul.

When Peter said he was in Babylon, I lean towards him actually going to Babylon and not like most scholars thinking he meant spiritual Babylon which is Rome.

I believe Peter meant what he said when he said that he went to Babylon. Rome doesn't become spiritual Babylon until the start of Thyatira which is when the bishop of Rome took the title Pontificus Maximus from the last Caesar. At Cyrus' decree to go to Jerusalem and build God's house, I learned from Dr.Scott that there were about 650,000 Jews living in Babylon and that just over 50,000 Jews went to Jerusalem.

Was there such a thing as Church and State in the wilderness journey? Yes. The leaders of the tribes that gave manna for the table of showbread had government authority which came from the devil. This giving of the manna didn't come from the saints (people). The devil will be in the abyss during the feast of tabernacles. The devil's angels will still rule on the earth during the feast of tabernacles through government. What shall be worshipped to the KING of kings will come from national leaders and for worshipping Jesus they will receive a blessing of rain and nothing more.

What can be said about the valley of Achor as a door of hope. I learned from Dr.Scott the plunder of Jericho was first fruits that went in the Lord's treasury. I believe the door is Jesus Christ. Jesus rose from the dead on the feast of first fruits. I believe the door is paying first fruits to the teacher of God's word. The thief in the flying scroll steals tithes and first fruits in the context of the Book of Malachi which is paying by promise.

I learned from Dr.Scott that the sun clothed woman in the Book of Revelation shall be the Israelites. The sun clothed woman is a distortion of Jacob's interpretation of Joseph's dream. In Jacob's interpretation, Rachel is the moon. The problem with that is Rachel was already dead when Jacob gave his interpretation. She died giving birth to Benjamin. Jacob was wrong.

During his ministry, Jesus made all other teachers of the Bible false teachers. During the Protestant Reformation, the chosen saints gave money to the chosen preachers. All Christians that didn't give money to the Protestant preachers went to hell. The Roman Catholic clergy that sold indulgences and that Pope didn't have their sins forgiven.

In the parable of tares and wheat, tares are false Christians. James and the Jerusalem Christians was the first false church. James was wrong in stating that Elijah prayed to stop the rain and to start the rain. Elijah never prayed this. Elijah stopped the rain by his word like Joshua stopped the sun. Joshua believed the sun went around the earth.

Joseph Smith, the founder of the Mormon Church asked for wisdom in the context of James' letter. Joseph Smith was a false Christian. The prophecy of the 144,000 is still yet to come. The Jehovah's witnesses are false Christians, they are not the 144,000.

Dr.Scott claimed his global ministry was the global ministry prophesied of in Zechariah 5:1-5:4. I know that the global prophecy in Revelation 3:10 is through the flying scroll, the global test was about paying tithes and Fisrtfruits to Dr.Scott. The prophecy of Revelation 3:10 ends the Philadelphia Church and is the start of the flying scroll and Laodicea a false church which is the Anglican Church.

Zechariah prophesied that two thirds of the Israelites will be dead by the end of the great tribulation. In one judgment in the Book of Revelation, one third of mankind will die which will be more than those that died in the flood. The Bible doesn't say what the 144,000 will do. I believe the 144,000 which will be in the lost tribe nations, for example: Canada and Australia, they will tell fellow Israelites what tribe they are from because Ezekiel prophesied that the remnant Israelites will repopulate their lots in Ancient Israel.

Jesus and John the Baptist were the only two teachers of the Bible. The Protestant preachers were the only chosen preachers of the Bible. Jesus made the flying scroll the only ministry that's allowed to teach the Bible rightly.

The mystery of Ezekiel 390 is as follows: God said in the Old Testament that if they didn't keep his covenant, he would punish them 7 times. Even though Ezekiel was sin bearer for both houses, God didn't forgive them of their sins. Ezekiel was suppose to be sin bearer representing 430 solar years. The Israelites were in Egypt for 430 solar years. Ezekiel lay on both sides for a total of 430 days and each day represented a year in Israel's history in Egypt. The House of Israel started to go into the Assyrian captivity in 721 B.C. From 721 B.C to 2010 A.D. is 7 x 390 solar years, Ezekiel lay on his left side for 390 days and each day represented a year times the seven times punishment also known as the seven times concealment of knowledge. In 2010 A.D., it wasn't that their sins were forgiven, Jesus made known by me in 2010 A.D. that Canada is Levi and Australia is Simeon. The mystery of Ezekiel 390 was revealed exactly on time. Even though Aaron confessed the sins of the Israelites onto the head of the escape goat, the majority of Israelites didn't have their sins forgiven because God swore in his wrath that they shall not enter into his rest. It was God's word of they shall not enter into my rest versus Aaron confessing the people's sins onto the head of the escape goat. It was God's word of there's no forgiveness of sins without the shedding of blood versus Ezekiel taking upon himself the sins of the Israelites. It was God's word of there's no forgiveness of sins without the shedding of blood that took precedence. On Passover, they all acted in faith by slaying the lambs. The thing is, very few were chosen, because God swore in his wrath that they shall not enter into his rest. Even though they all acted in faith in putting the booty of Jericho into God's treasury, very few were chosen. Dr.Scott taught, yesterday's faith is worth nothing, and I agree. He taught, it's how you finish. Put flesh and blood on the Bible, Ezekiel might of believed that because he was sin bearer, they would have their sins forgiven.

How I became a Christian. I was in my bedroom face down on the bed. I felt my butt cheeks spread and it was an invisible evil being that did this. I was terrorized. I was frightened. I prayed, If there's a God, help me. The following happened. I saw myself leaving my body. Immediately after this, I was an atheist and my soul was raptured into heaven and was in God's presence for about 5 minutes in the fetal position. Two days later, an angel or angels was in my bedroom. The bedroom lighted up very brightly. I tried opening my eyes but I was paralyzed. I was jabbed on the right side of my chest. This lasted a few seconds and the angel (s) took off. I never doubted since. I had a satellite dish. When I first listened to Dr.Scott, he was teaching on Adam Rutherford's book on the great pyramid. He said Jesus was born September 29, 2 B.C. This was shocking and got my attention. Dr.Scott started talking about me publicly in 1988 and did this for years. Dr.Scott prophesied about me. Dr.Scott gave me a copy right to his teaching before he died. He said to me on his T.V. broadcast, " You can use my teaching as long as you acknowledge your source". I have a conditional verbal copyright.

I had two encounters with evil beings, this was in 1992 or 1993. I was on my back in my bedroom. I felt a sensation come over me, I sensed an evil presence, all of a sudden there's an evil being touching the back of my head, this lasted about 3 seconds, my eyes were changed so that I can see in the invisible realm. I see an evil being about 18 inches in height and looked like a mass of gray dots, it leaves the room through the wall.

Next episode, I was in my apartment again at Marion Grocery. I sensed an evil presence. I sense a deep sense of danger. My mind was attacked by an evil being. I didn't know what to do. I decided to escape this by taking a trip to Miami, Florida. I was sitting pool-side at a Motel. All of a sudden I had a great sense of fear from an evil invisible being, this lasted a few seconds and all of sudden I see a black mass materialize about 200 feet away, then it disappeared. I was very scared from this encounter.

I agreed with over 99% of Dr.Scott's teaching. I don't agree with you (Pastor Melissa Scott) that Jesus was born on the feast of tabernacles. And I don't agree with you that the manna for the table of shewbread came from the saints in the Old Testament. I don't agree with Dr.Scott teaching that the manna for the table of shewbread represented giving from the saints. The manna for the table of shewbread came from the national leaders that had delegated authority from the devil. The offerings that will be worshipped to Jesus during the feast of tabernacles will be given in exchange for rain as a blessing and won't be like laying up treasures in heaven. As Samson killed one thousand men, Jesus for one thousand years will not give eternal life to those that will worship him during the feast of tabernacles. Those that will worship Jesus during the feast of tabernacles, I don't believe they will qualify as the saints in Christ Jesus, I believe the flying scroll will still be active during the feast of Tabernacles and the saints in Christ Jesus will pay tithes, firstfruits and give offerings that qualify as laying up treasures in heaven.

I learned from Dr.Scott that the booty of Jericho was the Firstfruits of the Old Testament and that it was a Sabbath when the children of Israel conquered Jericho. Achan and his family got the death penalty for stealing part of the Firstfruits. The door in the door of hope in the valley of Achor is Jesus Christ. The door is paying Firstfruits and don't be like Achan the thief. Why Joshua and the army was successful in taking city after city is because they paid Firstfruits.

Dr.Scott designated your income from January 1ˢᵗ to the 7ᵗʰ as the amount for paying Firstfruits for the year. Jesus promised that an angel will go before you and keep you in the way for paying firstfruits. If you want, you can pay on the feast of Firstfruits and make it your starting point. It would be the Sabbath during the feast of Unleavened Bread. Only the chosen saints in Christ Jesus will pay Firstfruits to Pastor Melissa Scott.

Rahab the harlot was the Firstfruits chosen from the heathen. She made it to the 11ᵗʰ chapter of Hebrews.

Years ago, Dr.Scott prophesied about me. A prophetess by the name of Clara Grace gave 5 prophecies about Dr.Scott. The 3ʳᵈ prophecy is easiest to demonstrate. She said, "God is going to take your voice and hurl it world-wide". Dr.Scott went world-wide on short wave radio live or on tape 24/7 in 1989, afterwards, he went world-wide on the internet 24/7 live or on tape. She gave these prophecies before 1975.

Dr.Scott claimed to be Elijah that Jesus prophesied of and that his ministry was the global ministry prophesied of in Zechariah 5:1-5:4. He was teaching on Elijah and said, " Hide thyself in Glendale", He was referring to himself in Glendale, California. He was teaching on the flying scroll and said, " A cursing satellite", Technically, a satellite is positioned over the middle of the U.S. and transmits up to Canada and Mexico.

What he meant was his global ministry. The thief in the flying scroll doesn't steal from his fellow man like some scholars have said, the thief steals from God and there's only one context for that, it's stealing from God tithes and firstfruits in the context of Malachi. Those that don't pay, God promises them death which is the second death in the Book of Revelation which is to be cast into the lake of fire. The prophecy of the flying scroll is so grand because it makes all other churches false churches.

Years ago, I wrote the following in a public essay: Jesus said, "Give to Caesar what is Caesar's and to God what is God's". What belongs to Caesar is taxes and what belongs to God is property rights which tithes and firstfruits in the context of Malachi. Jesus doesn't answer prayers from those that don't pay tithes and firstfruits. He doesn't answer prayers to the thief in the context of the flying scroll. I believe the King James translators were under Satan's control like most scholars today. I studied Greek. I have a Greek Bible.

Isaiah was the smartest person on the planet in his days as was the apostle Paul. A true teacher of God's word should be the smartest person on the planet, that's what Dr. Scott was. I believe Pastor Melissa Scott is the smartest person on the planet.

Moses thought he was speaking with God on top of Mount Sinai. Stephen and Paul said the law was given by angels. I remember Dr.Scott saying that it was Michael on top of Mount Sinai.

Part of Jesus' teaching was speaking forth new laws, for example, when he told a man to sell all that he had and give it to the poor, this was to obtain eternal life by a new law. Paul said that Christ has redeemed us from the curse of the law. This curse also applies to Jesus teaching new laws. Notice that giving less than 100% to the poor didn't qualify.

Abraham gave vertically to God by giving burnt offerings and gave horizontally by paying a tithe to Melchizedek. The first story I read in the Bible was chapter 11 of the Book of Revelation, the prophecy of the last two witnesses. Upon reading this, what came to mind was that Dr.Scott and I would be just as important as the last two witnesses. I think this was in 1988, I wanted special knowledge from Jesus and God. I was already giving regularly to Dr.Scott. I took $400.00 and burnt it as a sweet savor burnt offering so that I can receive revelations by Jesus Christ and God. I paid a $1000.00 vow to Dr.Scott. My vow was that my letters would be understood by the saints during the feast of tabernacles.

God didn't redeem nations. Samson killing one thousand men with the jawbone of a donkey is like Jesus rejecting the offerings that will be made to him by national leaders during the feast of tabernacles because this giving is like those leaders that supplied the manna for the table of showbread, this giving will be done by tares which are false Christians.

When two prophecies contradict one another, one has to take precedence. For example, Hosea prophesied not my people, my people and interpreted this as the House of Israel. Along came Peter and Paul and interpreted this prophecy as belonging to the saints in Christ Jesus. Another example is God's word of that there's no forgiveness of sins without the shedding of blood taking precedence over Ezekiel as sin bearer. Even though Ezekiel was suppose to be sin bearer, the Israelites didn't have their sins forgiven. Jesus' words of forgiving your brother 490 times wasn't about forgiving sins. Daniel's seventy weeks of years is 490 years. It was about time of concealed knowledge. The 29th chapter of Acts was published in 1800 A.D. From 721 B.C. which is when the House of Israel started the Assyrian captivity to 1800 A.D. is 7 x 360 solar years equals 1800 A.D. The 29 chapter of Acts was published exactly on time. Ezekiel laying on on his sides for 430 days and each day represented one year living in Egypt. Ezekiel on his left side for 390 days and each day represented a solar year. From 721 B.C., 7 x 390 solar years equals 2010 A.D. which is not about forgiving sins, it's about knowledge that Jesus revealed through me and it was that Canada is Levi and Australia is Simeon and I wrote about this publicly in 2010 which was exactly on time.

You might ask, how can Levi be a tribe when they lived among the Israelites in cities appointed for them. Jacob prophesied about them as a tribe. Another example is God's words of that they shall not enter into my rest versus Aaron confessing the sins of the Israelites onto the head of the escape goat and sprinkling the blood of the goat onto the mercy seat, the majority of Israelites didn't have their sins forgiven even though Aaron did his duty. What did the publication of the 29th chapter of Acts in 1800 A.D. do? It made known to British citizens that they were Israelites. What did the mystery of Ezekiel 390 revealed produce? It identified two Israelite nations, namely, Canada and Australia and that Canada was conquered by members of the tribe of Levi and that Australia was conquered by members of the tribe of Simeon.

In Hebrews 8:8, Paul says the house of Israel and the house of Judah. But in Hebrews 8:10, he doesn't mention the house of Judah. What happened? He made a mistake. I remember Dr.Scott teaching that when Jesus cursed the fig tree, he said that Jesus cursed the house of Judah. I believe he cursed both houses.

I believe Paul was wrong. I don't believe God made a new covenant with both houses wherein he forgives them of their sins. For the last two thousand years, the vast majority of both houses weren't chosen, very very few were chosen among the Israelites

In judges, there's a tragic story of a Levite and his concubine that gets raped and dies from men of the tribe of Benjamin. The Levite man shockingly cuts up his concubine into twelve parts and sends them to the twelve tribes of Israel.

The twelve tribes fought the Benjamites in God's name. In Judges 20:21, the twelve tribes gave no offerings to God and the tribe of Benjamin killed 22,000 Israelites. What I want you to see is that these 22,000 Israelites were not redeemed by God. In Judges 20:25, the Israelites again gave no offering to the Lord and 18,000 Israelites get killed by the Benjamites. These Israelites were not redeemed by God. 22,000 plus 18,000 equals 40,000 and that 40 I learned from Dr. Scott is the number of complete testing by God, In Judges 20:26, they go to Bethel and offer up burnt offerings to the Lord which is the right thing to do. In Judges 20:29, God promises them victory over the Benjamites and that's what happened. Forty thousand men died because they didn't give an offering before going to battle. The lesson is, if you go to war in God's name, you had better give offerings first.

In Revelation 3:10 is a prophecy of the global testing of paying tithes and firsfrutis to the domata of the flying scroll. The prophecy of the flying scroll is so grand because it makes all other churches false churches and because Jesus' feet are burnished bronze in Revelation, this means Jesus judged and condemned all other churches. I learned from Dr.Scott and scholars that bronze symbolized judgment.

In Romans 9:25, Paul interprets Hosea's prophecy as being the saints in Christ Jesus. In 9:27, he interprets the remnant of both houses as being the saints in Christ Jesus. How can he turn around in Hebrews and say that God made a new covenant with both houses unless he's wrong. He was wrong in the Hebrews letter concerning both houses. I don't believe God made a new covenant with both houses.

In chapter 11 of the Book of Revelation is the prophecy of the last two witnesses which are symbolically referred to as olive trees. These two olive trees are the same two olive trees that are in Zechariah and both prophecies are for the same time. In Revelation, the seven golden lampstands are the seven churches. Dr.Scott taught on the etymological meaning of the word church in Greek and it is "Out/called/ones". In the first century, a person walked down the street and called people out of their houses, there would be a purpose. The two olive trees will be Elijah and Moses in both books of Zechariah and Revelation. In Zechariah, these two olive trees are pouring olive oil which I learned from Dr.Scott symbolizes the Holy Spirit and pour into the golden lampstand which symbolized a new church during the first half of the great tribulation. Chapter 11 of Revelation and Revelation 4:1 start on the same day. This day I learned from Dr.Scott is the second half of the feast of the trumpets which is when the rapture takes place. The identify of the two olive trees and the identity of the antichrist will be revealed immediately after the rapture, It's prophesied that if anyone tries to hurt either Elijah or Moses, that fire will literally come out of their mouths and kill their enemies, this will be very miraculous to see this. There won't anymore atheists on the earth, all will know that God and Jesus exist. I don't believe the thief in the flying scroll gets his prayers granted. The thief in the flying scroll steals tithes and firstfruits from God's damata which now is Pastor Melissa Scott.

Jesus' words to Peter that you are to forgive your brother of his sin 490 times wasn't about forgiving sins, it was about the time of concealment of knowledge. Dr.Scott taught that why scholars are wrong in dating Daniel's seventy weeks is that they use the solar calendar instead of the 360 day a year calendar. I learned from Dr.Scott that it's Artaxerxes edict is the starting point of Daniel's seventy weeks of years and it is on a calender of 360 days a year. Messiah being cut off was 483 years at 360 days a year which brings the date to Passover 33 A.D. I learned from Dr.Scott that the last two witnesses in Revelation shall be Elijah and Moses. Their ministry will be for three and half years at 360 days a year which is 1260 days. God told Ezekiel that he would be sin bearer but that's not what happened. It was about concealment of knowledge, just like Jesus' words to Peter of forgiving your brother of his sins wasn't about forgiving sins it was about concealment of knowledge. Daniel's seventy weeks starts with Artaxerxes edict in 444 B.C and ends when Jesus returns as KING of kings. There's a gap of one week of 7 x 360 days for a 7 year period known as the great tribulation. The 360 days a year calendar will combine with the calendar of God's feast days which is the lunar calendar. They will combine when the rapture takes place. I know without a doubt that the rapture will take place exclusively through the flying scroll.

Melchizedek's ministry was like from the God of Jacob. Abraham paid a tithe just like Jacob did. The wine and bread that Melchizedek had was just like Jesus and his disciples with the elements of the communion table.

The Book of Malachi was a contrast of being blessed by paying tithes and firstfruits or being cursed for not paying. Only those that pay tithes and firstfruits to Pastor Melissa Scott are blessed by Jesus and the God.

During the wilderness journey, God swore in his wrath that they shall not enter into his rest. It didn't matter that Aaron confessed the sins of the Israelites onto the escape goat nor that he sprinkled the goat's blood onto the mercy seat seven times. Say what? Even though Aaron did his duty as high priest, the majority of the Israelites didn't have their sins forgiven because God swore they shall not enter into God's rest.

The Tabernacle was a meeting place between God and man. On the day of Atonement, God would sit as judge and evaluated the blood of a goat. The goat's blood could possibly forgiven sins for the past year. It was a temporary forgiveness of sins while the blood of the Passover Lamb could forgive sins eternally. When Jesus forgave the woman caught in the act of adultery, that was like the blood of a goat in value, she didn't have her eternal sins forgiven. She also didn't give Jesus an offering.

The Levitical priests were mediators between God and man. Paul said that the preacher of the gospel takes the place of the Levitical priest. Jesus and the God chose Dr.Scott to be his only voice to preach to the chosen saints. Now, the next teacher in the flying scroll is Pastor Melissa Scott.

Why there are so many child molesters in the Roman Catholic Church over the centuries is because they are false Christians.

Jesus referred to himself as the way. Peter described his death as his exodus. ex means out, and odus means way. Elijah and Moses in Greek described Jesus' his death as his exodus. Jesus died on the anniversary death as his exodus. I learned from Dr.Scott that Paul used the word departure to describe his own death and it described a ship just leaving the harbor.

Jesus said, God first to the lost sheep of the House of Israel. The gospel went out to them. Few of them became saints in Christ

Jesus while the vast majority were not chosen. In Hebrews. Paul mentions a new covenant of forgiving sins for the House of Israel and the House of Judah. He only mentions the House of Israel. What happened? He made a mistake.

Dr.Scott was too proud to take correction. After I told him that he was wrong in stating that Laodicea wasn't the false church, he turned around and said pain and Cain. To his statement of pain, I wrote that pain in French is bread. What I meant by this is his statement of pain I didn't believe would happen and it didn't. Either Dr.Scott or you (Pastor Melissa Scott) are right on when Jesus was born. I learned from Dr.Scott that silver symbolized redemption. I agree with Dr.Scott that Jesus was born on the feast of the trumpets. I don't agree with Pastor Melissa Scott that Jesus was born on the feast of tabernacles. This doesn't makes sense as to when Jesus was born. Zechariah prophesied of the feast of tabernacles as still yet to come, therefore, Jesus couldn't have been born of the feast of tabernacles. Both you (Pastor Melissa Scott) and Dr.Scott were wrong in stating that Paul went to the 3rd heaven when Paul clearly was talking about another person going to the 3rd heaven. Both you and Dr.Scott were wrong in teaching that the manna given by the leaders of the nations of Israel symbolized giving by the saints when clearly it wasn't the saints giving this manna. Dr.Scott made several mistakes. Tithing is righteous behavior, it makes one right with God and Jesus. Dr.Scott taught that tithing doesn't make you righteous. Joseph's dream existed for over thousands of years. Nobody else pointed out that Rachel was dead when Joseph had his dream and that Rachel can't be the moon. Joseph was simply wrong and the sun-clothed woman is a distortion of Joseph's dream. What actually happened? I was studying Joseph's dream. I heard a voice in my head say to me, Rachel can't be the moon because she was dead when Joseph had his dream. I find it hard to swallow that you (Pastor Melissa Scott) said Rachel was spiritually alive. I believe Jesus revealed this to me just like he revealed to me that Laodicea is the Anglican church and is a false church and that Thyatira is the false church. When I went to King's House 1 years ago, after I got back home, Dr.Scott said about me, Antichrist came to town. Why he said this, I don't know. He was simply wrong. One time, he was sitting with his bible on his lap, he like sign languaged to me to write a letter publicly to inform him what I knew. Dr.Scott was right in stating that I shouldn't give out knowledge for free. When I wrote my first public letter, I thought it would be my only letter. By writing public letters, I had hoped to turn some people around get them to follow Dr.Scott. It was Jesus that revealed to me that the rapture will take place exclusively through the flying scroll. It was Jesus that revealed to me that Revelation 3:10 is the flying scroll and that the global testing prophesied of is tithes and firstfruits that was payable to Dr.Scott and now to you (Pastor Melissa Scott). More than once I thought I would be a preacher, but it's not to be. I'm a student of Greek, not a teacher of Greek. After the rapture takes place, the flying scroll's congregation will have ascended. This is when the last two witnesses will start a new church. I believe the flying scroll will also start a new church, it will be in the land of the wilderness for the sun-clothed woman. The wilderness that the sun-clothed woman flees to in Revelation will be the geography of the United States because it's the only nation wherein their Bill of Rights is not subject to government authority. I believe only thousands will become saints during the great tribulation, it won't be millions. How many will be chosen is predetermined just like how many will take the mark of the beast is predetermined. How many pay tithes and firsfruits to Pastor Melissa Scott is predetermined by the Lord and God. I think Aaron cast the rod before the children of Israel and it became a serpent. It might be, that Moses didn't put his hand into his bosom and it became leprous, I don't know if he did this sign in front of the Israelites. Maybe only the first sign was performed.

Over 99% of the religious people were wrong in worshipping in the Old Testament, the New Testament and I believe it will be same for the feast of tabernacles. In Revelation, the devil will be cast into the abyss. I don't know for sure, I think the devil's angels will still rule through government during the feast of tabernacles. There was a thing as church and state during the wilderness journey. The national leaders of the tribes that supplied the manna for the table of showbread had delegated authority from the devil. This manna didn't represent giving to God from individuals. I don't believe what shall be worshipped to Jesus during the feast of tabernacles will be laying up treasures in heaven. I believe this giving will receive rain in exchange and nothing more. If they don't worship, there will be no rain and if done again, then a plague.

Pastor Melissa Scott is now the global curser in the flying scroll. If anyone doesn't pay tithes and firstfruits to Pastor Melissa Scott, you're a thief in the prophecy of the flying scroll, therefore, test Jesus in your prayers, if you're a thief, you won't get your prayers answered. For paying tithes and firstfruits, God promises a blessing in the here and now. Going beyond that, you are laying up treasures in heaven and promised a future blessing.

Pastor Melissa Scott taught that WWW in Hebrew is 666. The Sabbath was at the end of the 6th day. Dr.Scott taught that 6 is the number of a man. Adam was created on the 6th day. I learned from Dr.Scott that 3 is the number of divine manifestation. 666 is the devil's man manifested. The word mark in the mark of the beast is transliterated as ikon. A picture on a dollar bill is its ikon. The antichrist's ikon is 666. Jesus fulfilled the number 6 by being the Lord of the Sabbath and Paul in the Hebrews letter changed the Sabbath into a function of acting on any promise of God in the Bible. Jesus was raised from the dead at the end of the 6th day fulfilling the Sabbath. How close are we to the mark of the beast? The mark (icon) of the beast will be some form of microchip or RFID chip implanted in the right hand or the forehead. In the farming industry, it's now normal and accepted practice to microchip animals which is a slow brainwashing that microchipping is progressive thinking. Revelation says the mark of the beast will be able to speak. Microchips can speak when scanned by infrared light at checkout counters which is a prototype of the mark.

Revelation 12:3 And another portent appeared in heaven; behold a great red dragon, with seven heads and ten horns, and seven diadems upon his heads.

The seven heads are seven kings. The 6th head was the Caesar at the time John was receiving revelations The 7th head shall be the antichrist. The ten horns shall be the antichrist's ten nations kingdom. I learned from Dr.Scott that the first 6 beastly kingdoms are: Egypt; Assyria; Babylon; Medo-Persia; Greece; and the Roman Empire. In Revelation 13:2 the leopard refers to Greece and its bear feet is the geography of Medo-Persia while mouth of a lion refers to Babylon's message.

In Revelation 13:3 the head that had a mortal wound is the evil invisible being that possessed Alexander The Great that was now in the abyss. And its mortal wound that was healed means this invisible being came out of the abyss and now possessed the antichrist.

The 42 months in Revelation 13:5 is 30 day months. It's the same calendar as the last two witnesses. The last two witnesses in chapter 11 shall be Elijah and Moses and their prophecies will be for 1260 days which is 42 x 30 day months which is three and a half years.

In Revelation 13:14, the beast is the invisible being that possessed Alexander The Great, the wound is that invisible being after it possessed Alexander The Great, its wound was that it was placed into the abyss again and the words "yet lived" means that invisible being now lived in the antichrist.

In Revelation17:6 the words " it was" refers to the invisible being that possessed Alexander The Great and the words " is not" refers to that being being in the abyss and the words " is to come" means that it will posses the antichrist.

In Revelation 17:9, the seven heads are the seven heads of the beastly kingdoms and the seven mountains are the seven beastly kingdoms with the 7th mountain being the ten toed kingdom prophesied by Daniel which is the ten horned kingdom in the Book of Revelation.

In Revelation17:10 the seven kings are the heads of the seven beastly kingdoms. The five that have fallen are the king of Egypt; Assyria; Babylon; Medo-Persia; Greece and the "one is" is the Caesar at the time John receiving revelations and the one not yet come is the antichrist with his ten horned beastly kingdom.

In Revelation 17:11 the difference between the 7th and 8th is the 7th is the antichrist during the first half of the great tribulation which will be his ten horned kingdom and the 8th is the antichrist with the invisible being out of the abyss possessing him during the second half of the great tribulation and global authority over governments.

Scholars claim that the seven hills of Rome are the seven mountains in the Book of Revelation. They're wrong. Scholars claim that the antichrist's ten horned kingdom will be a revived Roman Empire, yet there's no evidence to suggest that in the book or Revelation nor in the book of Daniel. It says, the seven heads are seven mountains. The seven heads are not the seven hills of Rome. Dr.Scott taught from the book of Daniel and said the antichrist comes out the Seleucid Empire which is modern day Syria. The antichrist will be an Arab. More than likely, the ten horned kingdom will all Arab nations. In Daniel, the antichrist wars against three nations and becomes their head and seven other nations given him their authority and this will give him authority over ten nations. The 7th head is the antichrist and the 7th mountain is the antichrist's ten horned kingdom. It's said in Revelation that the 7 heads are 7 mountains, the seven heads are the seven kings of the beastly kingdoms and the seven mountains are the seven beastly kingdoms. The first beastly kingdom was Egypt, when a Pharaoh that knew not Joseph rose up and put the Israelites into slavery.

The 144,000 in the Book of Revelation are in Revelation 7:1-7:8 and Revelation 14:1-5. The 144,000 will preach to scattered Israelites throughout the scattered lost tribe nations and then be raptured horizontally like Philip was raptured and this will be to Mount Zion and after will be raptured into heaven. The 144,000 will preach to Israelites and tell them which tribe they are from so that they can repopulate the ancient land of Israel because it's prophesied by Ezekiel that they will have their lots reassigned to them. The 144,000 will preach to Israelites that rejected the mark of the beast and weren't beheaded, these Israelites will be survivors, they will be alive when Jesus returns as KING of kings.

In Revelation 7:1-7:8 the 144,000 are scattered in the so called lost tribes nations.

In Revelation 14:1, the 144,000 are at Mount Zion, how were they gathered together? They were raptured horizontally from the so called lost tribe nations to Mount Zion. In Revelation 14:2 the 144,000 are singing in heaven, what happened? They were raptured from Mount Zion into heaven.

Who will build Ezekiel's Temple? Will it be Jews only or will the builders come from all 12 tribes? In Solomon's Temple, the builders came from all 12 tribes.

From the scattering of people at the time of the tower of Babel, do you think the Indians living in the Americas came from Babel. The people of China have dragon parades, what can this be traced to? At Babel, the planets and stars was worshipped and was their religion. At that time, the northern star was Alpha Draconis, the dragon star symbolizing the devil.

I learned from Dr.Scott that the United States is the tribe of Manasseh, that the British Empire is the tribe of Ephraim, that the French is the tribe of Benjamin, that Denmark get its name from Dan of the tribe of Dan, that Danites founded Ireland. I also learned from him that when a Pharaoh that knew not Joseph that there was an exodus by sea. Members of the tribe of Judah left Egypt and settled in Spain. Jeremiah disappears from the bible and has the two daughters of Zedekiah with him, he drops off one daughter in Spain and has her marry the Melitian king, they were both of the tribe of Judah. Spain conquered South America and Mexico, they are descendants of Judah. He also taught that the Celtic nations are the tribes of Israel. The mystery of Ezekiel that Jesus revealed through me is that Canada is Levi and Australia is Simeon.

Jesus made preachers as mediators between himself and the saints in Christ Jesus. What about money? Pastor Melissa Scott is the global curser in the flying scroll. I wrote years ago that the global ministry of testing in Revelation 3:10 is the flying scroll. In the flying scroll, if you don't pay, God promises spiritual death which is the second death in Revelation which is to be cast into the lake of fire.

Enoch's life was one solar year as a day in his life. Ezekiel was appointed a 390 year calendar. Jeremiah was appointed 3 feasts in Ireland.

Zachaeus was a legalist. In the law, if someone stole a sheep, they were to pay four fold. Most of those that Jesus taught weren't chosen. I don't believe Zacheus was chosen.

Can you see that Levi and Simeon were righteous for killing the rapist and those men that supported the rapist. Jacob was wrong for cursing their anger.

When the widow with two mites put her money into the treasury, the temple was no longer God's place of worship. The Ethiopian Eunuch put money into this same treasury and it also had no eternal value because it wasn't giving to God. The Ethiopian Eunuch didn't give money to Philip. I don't believe the widow and the Ethiopian eunuch were chosen.

I remember you (Pastor Melissa Scott) saying that we're partly in Philadelphian and partly in Laodicea. I don't know what scripture you were thinking of for saying that. The seven churches in Revelation have something said that starts or ends that individual church. I wrote to you (Pastor Melissa Scott) before stating when particular churches started. For example, Satan's throne in the Pergamus church was about the Emperor Constantine, that church started at the Council at Nicaea. I mentioned the global prophecy of testing through Dr.Scott's global ministry of the flying scroll, Revelation 3:10 is the ending of Philadelphia. Revelation 3:10 is Dr.Scott going world-wide on short wave radio. We can't be in Philadelphia and in Laodicea. Laodicea is a false church and is the Anglican church. Sardis was the Reformation church and started when Martin Luther nailed his 95 thesis to the door. Jezebel in Thyatira is a parable of the bishop of Rome. Thyatira started when the bishop of Rome took the title Pontificus Maximus from the last Caesar. Jesus promised to give Thyatira death. Thyatira is the harlot woman and Mystery Babylon and is the Roman Catholic Church. Dr.Scott taught that ten days in that Satan will cast you into prison was a parable of ten persecutions in the Smyrna church, there were ten government edicts against Christians. Ephesus starts when Jesus was raised from the dead and preached to Mary first. In the Ephesus letter, they're told that they abandoned their first love of Jesus and told to change their minds or else. John was the apostle of love in his letters and the church of Ephesus ends at his death.

Two of the seven start dates for churches in Revelation are dated in the great pyramid. I learned from Dr.Scott that the ceiling of the descending passage, it's bottom, the date is October 31, 1517, which is when Martin Luther nailed his 95 thesis to the door, which is the start date of Sardis. Another date is when Jesus was raised from the dead on the feast of firstfruits 33 A.D., this is when the grand gallery opens up with seven tiers, this date is when the Ephesus church started. The seven tiers represents the seven churches in Revelation.

The apostle Paul said Christ has redeemed us from the curse of the law. This curse should also apply to some of Jesus' teaching when he taught a new law. Jesus changed the old law of thou shalt not kill and made a new law that was, " If you hate in your heart, you are as guilty as a murderer." This was a new law that was a curse and it died and ended at calvary and not to be mimicked. Jesus spoke forth a new law which was a curse and died and ended at calvary when he taught to love your enemies. We can't love our enemies the devil and his angels and those they control. Christ Jesus set us free from loving our enemies. The parable of the good Samaritan was a new law, it wasn't behavior that the saints in Christ Jesus should mimic. The parable of the good Samaritan was a new law that defined who your neighbor was by law and suppose to help by law, thank God and Jesus that charity died with Jesus at calvary. Another new law that was a curse and ended and died at calvary was, Do onto others what you want done to you. It was a law and something that is not to be mimicked. Laying up treasures in heaven was a command that wasn't a new law. In the Book of Revelation, it's prophesied that the saints that will be beheaded will pray for vengeance against their enemies, they won't love the false prophet and the antichrist nor those that will behead them. Another new law by Jesus was to sell all that you have and give it to poor and then follow Jesus. Notice that giving less than 100% to charity didn't qualify.

Paul said Jesus was the substance of the feast days. Paul was partly wrong.

Jesus didn't fulfill Pentecost and won't fulfill the Day of Atonement. The Day of Atonement will be fulfilled by the two cherubims in the veil which is the last two witnesses Elijah and Moses during the first half of the great tribulation. I believe Passover was from the God of Jacob while the Day of Atonement was from the God of Israel. The escape goat received the sins of the Israelites but not the Egyptians for example. The blood of the Day of Atonement goat forgave sins for one year and was only for Israelites. It couldn't redeem a person like Rahab or Ruth. Jesus Christ as the Passover Lamb redeemed out of every ethnic group.

The Book of Revelation reveals that the ten horned beastly kingdom lead by the antichrist will burn with fire in one day the harlot woman (the mother of harlots church) which is Mystery

Babylon which is the false church which is the Roman Catholic Church which is headed in Vatican City. It can only be a nuclear weapon that destroys Vatican City. It's Revelation 17:16 that has this prophecy and in Revelation 17:18, it's the Pope that rules over the kings of the earth. The people prophesied of in Revelation 18:4 shall be Roman Catholics. The blood of martyrs is and shall be found in the Roman Catholic Church.

The devil offered Jesus all the kingdoms of the earth which is the title KING of kings. Dr.Scott taught that the medical profession and universities are under Satan's control. Psychiatry is a dangerous pseudo-science. Psychiatric drugs cause chemical imbalances; they cause neurons to fire or prevent neurons from firing which affects the patient in a bad way. It was in the 1960's or 70's that psychiatrists first diagnosed their patients as having a chemical imbalance without doing a chemical test nor any biological test. I believe some psychiatric patients are demon possessed. Psychiatric patients that hear a voice or voices talking to them are hearing a demon. Psychiatrists claim those that hear a voice are not actually hearing a voice and are diagnosed as having a hallucination. I believe some Psychiatrists are demon possessed. Dr.Scott taught that psychology is a poor excuse as a discipline. There are good videos by doctors on the web stating that psychiatry is a pseudo-science. Demons can be religious people. A demon is first encountered in the gospels worshipping God in a synagogue.

A holistic dentist will tell you that amalgams also known as silver fillings contain mercury which is a toxic poison. About half of regular dentists still put in silver fillings. I had 10 amalgams (mercury,silver fillings) replaced by white enamel. I read an article about a woman that was diagnosed with chron's disease. She couldn't figure out why she all of sudden felt tired and had no energy. Sure enough, she read an article about mercury fillings and thought this might be her problem. She got the mercury fillings replaced, she regained her strength, she was no longer tired and no longer diagnosed as having chron's disease. There are short videos and essays on the web showing the vapors that come out of mercury fillings. The vapors rise from the mouth and into the brain area, scary stuff. When I visited the holistic dentist and his assistant, he would take out no more than 3 fillings at a time. They would wear gas masks for the procedure so that the fumes of drilling the mercury out wouldn't affect them.

The fire in Zechariah 13:9 is the great tribulation. One third of the Israelites will be survivors of the great tribulation while two thirds will die and go to hell. This one third will be the sun-clothed woman. I learned from Dr. Scott that the sun-clothed womnan will be the Israelites. The man chlld will be raptured. The seed of this woman, the devil will war against. These Israelites will reject the mark of the beast and will be beheaded.

Paul wasn't all things to all men. He simply made a mistake. Only Jesus can say that he had no lineage nor natural father. Paul was wrong in stating that Melchizedek was without lineage and without father. He simply made a mistake just like Joseph was wrong In his dream. Just like Jacob was wrong in interpreting Rachel as the moon in Joseph's dream and you (Pastor Melissa Scott) were wrong in saying that Jesus was born of the feast of tabernacles. I agree with Dr.Scott that Jesus was born on the feast of the trumpets.I believe Abraham was previously taught to pay tithe by Shem and when he met Melchizedek which was Shem, he paid a tithe not to a stranger.

I have a copy of "The Illustrious Lineage Of The Royal House Of Britian". In it, it chronicles the kings and queens in succession the monarchs from Jacob's son Judah up to Queen Elizabeth II. When the queen got crowned, there was a rock underneath the coronation chair. This rock is called Jacob's pillar, also Jacob's pillow, also, the stone of scone. In Genesis, Jacob put his head on a rock to fall asleep, he named the rock Bethel which means Beth as house and el as God which was the house of God. I learned from Dr. Scott that Jeremiah took the rock from Palestine to Ireland. When Prince Charles gets coronated, that rock will be underneath the coronation chair. You can do a web search to get more information on Jacob's pillar. All these kings and queens had delegated authority from the devil. Solomon had delegated authority from the devil and was governed by the God of Jacob. When David and Bathsheba committed their sin, God wouldn't allow an animal to be sacrificed to appease God of his anger.

God gave them free manna for forty years. Jesus was like the God of Israel when he fed the 5,000 plus with free food. Their reaction to this miracle was to try and make him king in Israel.

When I first listened to Dr .Scott, he was teaching on Adam Rutherford's book on the great pyramid, the pyramid is prophesied of in Isaiah 19:19 and dates Jesus' birth at September 29th 2 B.C.. To learn when Jesus was born using the new testament, you can do a web search with the following words: Jesus born September, course of Abia. There are good essays on the subject matter. The devil deceived you if you believe Jesus was born December 25th

Isaiah 19:19 is as follows: In that day shall there be an altar to the LORD in the midst of the land of Egypt, and a pillar at the border thereof to the LORD,

How can there be an altar in the midst of Egypt and a pillar at its border at the same time? The following will explain this mystery.

There were two Egypts in Egypt's history, there was a lower and upper Egypt. One crown looked like a bowling pin while the other looked like a bowling pin holder. When one king rules both Egypts, the bowling pin crown was placed inside the bowling pin holder crown and the altar in the midst of Egypt was the great pyramid. When two kings ruled both Egypts, the pillar at the border of both Egypts was the great pyramid.

Words I might want to hear at my funeral. Peter in Greek described his upcoming death as his exodus. Elijah and Moses described Jesus' death as his exodus. Ex means out and odus means way. Jesus said, I'm the way. Jesus said you live by dying. For paying firstfruits, Jesus promised to send his angel to keep you in the way. In the first century, christianity was called the way. I learned from Dr.Scott that Paul described his death as his departure which described a ship just leaving the harbor.

I learned from Dr.Scott that the United States' Bill Of Rights is not subject to government authority. The First Amendment is as follows: Congress shall make no law respecting an establishment of religion, or prohibiting the free exercise thereof; or abridging the freedom of speech, or of the press or of the right of the people peaceably to assemble, and to petition the Government for a redress of grievances.

Canada's Charter of Freedoms and Rights is subject to government authority.

The Canadian Charter of Rights and Freedoms guarantees the rights and freedoms set out in it subject only to reasonable limits prescribed by law as can be demonstrably justified in a free and democratic society.

The words " subject; to; law" are in the text, which means the rights are not guaranteed nor are the freedoms but are subject to law.

God didn't and won't redeem nations. Samson killing one thousand men with the jawbone of a donkey is like Jesus rejecting the offerings that will be made to him by national leaders during the feast of tabernacles because this giving is like those leaders that supplied manna for the table of showbread, this giving will be done by tares. The national leaders that will worship the KING of kings during the feast of tabernacles, their nation will receive a blessing of rain and nothing more.

I remember Dr.Scott teaching on the mystery of the 153 fish. He said, "On the day of Pentecost, 17 languages are mentioned associated with their geographies." Peter spoke in tongues, they heard in 17 different languages. Dr.Scott revealed that if you add the numbers 1 through 17 it equals 153. $1 + 2 + 3 + 4 + 5 + 6 + 7 + 8 + 9 + 10 + 11 + 12 + 13 + 14 + 15 + 16 + 17 = 153$. The roof of the grand gallery in the pyramid is 153 sacred cubits. The parable of the 153 fish was a prophecy of the church, there were good fish and bad fish. the parable of tares and wheat was a parable of the church, they would grow at the same time. The false church started with James heading the Jerusalem church. Next in the false church is the Council of Nicaea, how many bishops were chosen by Jesus I don't know. The next stage of the false church is when the bishop of Rome took the title Pontificus Maximus from the last Caesar which is the start of Thyatira, Jesus promised this church death.

After the seven day feast of tabernacles, the eighth day was a high day Sabbath, I believe this day will be the judgment seat of Christ Jesus wherein rewards are handed out and positions to start out eternity will be granted.

The Book of Revelation reveals that the ten horned beastly kingdom lead by the antichrist will burn with fire in one day the harlot woman which is Mystery Babylon which is the false church which is the Roman Catholic Church which is headed in Vatican City. It can only be a nuclear weapon that destroys Vatican City. It's Revelation 17:16 that has this prophecy and in Revelation 17:18, it's the Pope that rules over the kings of the earth. The people prophesied of in Revelation 18:4 shall be Roman Catholics. The blood of martyrs will be found in the Roman Catholic Church. Jesus nor the new testament Christians wore religious clothing. It was Constantine that got the bishops to wear pagan religious clothing. The mitres that the Pope, the Cardinals and the Archbishop of Canterbury wear can be traced to Babylon and Egypt. In Alexander Hislop's book, "The two Babylons", there's a pagan Egyptian priest that wears a fish suit. The mitre represents the mouth of a fish. The Philistines worshipped a fish god named Dagon. Dr. Scott taught that the round wafer that catholics call the body of Christ actually comes from heathen priestesses in Egypt baking cakes to the Queen of heaven Ashtarte also known as Easter. Rabbits at Easter comes from the fertility cult of the Queen of Babylon Easter also known as Ashtarte. The apostle Peter was married. Catholic priests take a vow of celibacy which is wrong. The religion of the Roman Catholic church comes from a combination of the religions of the beastly kingdoms and/or distortions of these religions. For example, in Alexander Hislop's book the two Babylons, it's recorded that Lent which catholics practice comes from 40 days weeping for Tammuz. Why would Jews have Tammuz as one of their months? They absorbed the Babylonian calendar in the Babylonian captivity. Tammuz was born December 25. Jeremiah condemned them for cutting a tree out of the forest and decking it with gold and silver, hence the Christmas tree comes from Babylon. Throughout their history and today, the majority of Israelites followed one or more pagan religions.

King Henry the 8th was under Satan's control when he created the Anglican Church. The Queen is the head of the Anglican Church.

The Anglican Church is Laodicea and is a false church. The Queen has delegated authority from the devil and has the right to make the laws. King Solomon had delegated authority from the devil. King Solomon was governed by the God of Jacob while the Queen is governed by the God of Israel. The Queen is no preacher, she doesn't collect tithes, firstfruits nor offerings from any saint.

James 5:17 Elijah was a man of like nature with ourselves and he prayed fervently that it might not rain, and for three years and six months it did not rain on the earth. 5:18 Then he prayed again and the heaven gave rain, and the earth brought forth its fruit.

James was wrong in inventing this.

Elijah didn't pray for the rain to stop. Elijah didn't pray for the rain to start again. Elijah had no foreknowledge that it would be for three and half years. God told Elijah that it would rain. Elijah stopped the rain by his word just like Joshua stopped the sun by his word. Joshua believed the sun went around the earth. I remember Dr.Scott teaching that Elijah prayed that God would stop the rain. Dr.Scott was deceived by James' letter. Dr.Scott simply made a rare mistake like Paul. I mentioned before that one of Dr.Scott's mistake was to say in the University Pulpit that Laodicea is the false church.

The Roman Catholic Church is the mother of harlots in Revelation. The prophecy of the flying scroll is so grand because it makes all other churches harlots. The exception will be the two olive trees in Zechariah which are Elijah and Moses and they will pour into the golden lampstand which shall be a new church during the first half of the great tribulation.

Why would I mention that I gave money to Dr.Scott on a regular basis when Matthew 6 says that we are to give in secret? Because the Bible records Abraham giving a tithe to Melchizedek and records his offerings and that the book of Jasher records Jacob paying his tithe vow to his son Levi. I listened to Dr.Scott from 1988 till he died. I must of listened to over 50,000 hours of his teaching until 2005. I"m proud to say that he watched over my soul. Dr.Scott explained more mysteries about the Bible than the apostle Paul. Dr.Scott taught from Hebrew and Greek material.

My parents died a few years ago. They were Roman Catholics. They were typical Christians, they never read a Bible from cover to cover. I believe they were put in hell and on judgment day will cast into the lake of fire.

The Bible records that Esau and King Zedekiah were profane. I learned from Dr.Scott that profanity has to with not discerning the true nature of spiritual things. Esau's profanity was that he sold his birthright. King Zedekiah's profanity is that he didn't believe Jeremiah's prophecy nor Ezekiel's. Jeremiah prophesied Zedekiah would be taken as prisoner to Babylon. Ezekiel wrote a letter to Zedekiah which said he won't see Babylon. Upon this knowledge, King Zedekiah had a meeting with his counsellors. They concluded that both prophets were liars because their prophecies contradicted one another. The king of Babylon invaded Jerusalem and Zedekiah fled to Riblah. At Riblah, they took the eyes out of his head and took him prisoner to Babylon. Jeremiah's prophecy came to pass as did Ezekiel's prophecy. I learned from Josephus' book, "Antiquity of the Jews", that God set a trap for King Zedekiah.

In Genesis 49:11, what is meant by, he will wash his garments in wine, his robes in the blood of grapes? Armageddon. In Luke 17:34 what is meant that they will be taken? A horizontal rapture. In Luke 17:37, the place they are gathered is Armageddon. In Revelation 14:17-20 the place of the great winepress is the plains of Megiddo prophesied by Ezekiel which is Armageddon. Those that received the mark of the beast will hated by God and Jesus and will be raptured from all over the earth to Armageddon and be killed by Jesus Christ.

Dr.Scott taught that there are 203 offerings associated with the feast of Tabernacles. The pyramid which was built I believe by Enoch and has 203 courses of masonry.

The prophecy of the flying scroll which started when Dr.Scott went world-wide of short wave radio is also the start of Revelation 3:10 which ends the church of Philadelphia. The flying scroll started at the sametime as Laodicea which is a false church which is the Anglican church. The Queen is a false apostle like the Pope. Peter wasn't the first Pope like catholics claim. Peter was dressed like a fishermen with a small sword. The first Pope was when the bishop of Rome took the title Pontificus Maximus from the last Caesar.

These last days are the days of the 6th beastly kingdom which started with Julius Caesar and the Roman Empire. I believe 9/11 was an inside job orchestrated by the Bush family and the owner of the twin towers. The government of the United States and the British Empire are part of the 6th beastly kingdom which is part of the Roman Empire prophesied by Daniel and John. There are several websites reporting that the government of the United States purchased 30,000 guillotines. I don't know if this is true. The Book of Revelation specifically says that the saints will be beheaded for rejecting the mark of the beast. The Book of Daniel says that the little horn which is the antichrist will war against the king of the south which is Egypt, this will be infighting in the devil's kingdom. All the soldiers that fought in the two world wars had delegated authority from the devil, it was in fighting in the devil's kingdom. These Christian soldiers that died in these wars were false Christians, because they didn't lay up treasures in heaven. These soldiers were not biblical heroes, they were heroes of the world which said world is God damned.

In Malachi in the KJV, God demands tithes and offerings which is not accurate. The Septuagint is accurate, it's tithes and firstruits.

Artists for centuries painted angels with wings. The bible doesn't picture angels with wings. When Gabriel visited Daniel and Mary he didn't have wings. The beings with wings are cherubs. I believe it was part of God's poetry to picture cherubs with wings so that man can understand that cherubs can fly compared to man. I believe the two cherubs at the door of the garden of Eden might have been Michael and Gabriel standing in for Elijah and Moses the last two witness in Zechariah and Revelation. The word arch in archangel refers to a title in relation to God. The cherubims Elijah and Moses are the two highest ranking angels/messengers in relation to God and Jesus. Paul referred to himself as an angel/messenger.

I believe the shroud of Turin is authentic. When the antichrist destroys Mystery Babylon with a nuclear weapon, I hope the shroud will survive the blast.

In the parable of the new wine must be put into new wine skins. The new wine was Paul's message of Grace and Peace.

I'll mention this again. A prophecy. The rapture will take place exclusively through the flying scroll. After the rapture, the last two witnesses will start a new church and make all other churches harlots except the flying scroll. Paul said, All Asia has forsaken me, only Luke is with me. Paul was referring to Christians that didn't want to associate with him.

Fulfilled prophecy brings confidence that Jesus is in control and that he can be trusted to bring to pass prophecies yet to come. The prophecy of the 30 pieces of silver that Judas was paid was prophesied by Zechariah. The book of Zechariah has the prophecy that the feast of Tabernacles will be from year to year, it's the book of Revelation that says Jesus' kingdom will be for one thousand years. It shouldn't be surprising that Dr.Scott's global ministry was prophesied of in Zechariah 5:1-5:4 and Revelation 3:10. Jesus said the gospel will be preached to all nations before the end comes, remember, the last two witnesses Elijah and Moses will start a new church. It's Elijah and Moses prophesied of in Zechariah 7:11-7:14, the golden lampstand shall be their new church.

Jesus's parable of Jonah technically wasn't a sign that he would raise from the dead. It was that he would be dead for 72 hours. He rose from the dead technically after this parable. I remember Dr.Scott teaching about Good Friday and Easer which isn't 72 hours. He said, Friday comes into the English language from a Scandinavian source called good freyla and was the

Scandinavian name for the Queen of Babylon named Ashtarte hence the name Easter. I remember Dr.Scott teaching that Jesus died on a Wednesday and rose from the dead on the Sabbath day which was the feast of firstfruits and that it was Saturday sundown which is when the day starts in the Bible. I think it's in Alexander Hislop's book the two Babylons that I learned that noon and midnight, dividing the day and night this way, comes from Babylon. The names of the week in the French are as follows; Monday is moon day. Tuesday is mars day. Wednesday is mercury day. Thursday is Jupiter day. In English, Saturday means saturn day and Sunday means sun day.

God was a polygamist. He was married to Oholah and Oholibah, they were both whores. He divorced the House of Israel and punished the House of Judah. The mother of harlots is the Roman Catholic Church. The harlot children are false churches.

In Revelation 4:1, John hears a voice like the sound of a trumpet. Jesus was speaking using a symbol. I learned from Dr.Scott that the rapture will take place on the second half of the feast of the trumpets. I learned from Dr.Scott that on the feast of the trumpets, two silver trumpets were sounded all day long with silver symbolizing redemption. He described the two trumpets splitting like, looking at a mountain top as one silver trumpet and not until reaching the summit that it's revealed to see another mountain top with a valley in between with the valley as the time between the two silver trumpets. As mentioned before, Jesus was born of the feast to the trumpets which is based a lunar calendar.

I learned from Dr.Scott that 4 is the number of the world. The four craftsmen in Zechariah was Dr.Scott and the four horns was Senator Petris in signing the Petris Bill which freed all churches in the United States from government inspecting churches in their money offerings to them. I learned from Dr.Scott that prior to the Petris Bill, the government said that churches are charitable trusts and are under the authority of the attorney general. Dr.Scott said that churches are not charitable trusts but a church can chose to be a charitable trust.

In Revelation 2:5, the Ephesus church is warned that if it didn't repent, Jesus would remove its lampstand which symbolized that church. What's written for one church in Revelation was said and applied to all seven churches. Thyatira and Laodicea had their lampstands removed because they didn't believe Revelation 3:10 which is about the flying scroll.

In Revelation 14:6-7 is a global prophecy through a global ministry and says it will at the time of God's judgment nearing, which places this prophecy as to sometime during the great tribulation and will come from the preacher of the flying scroll or some other new ministry to come of the scene.

James was a tare, he founded the first false church in Jerusalem. James said, resist the devil and he will flee from you. James was wrong. There were 10 martyred apostles and the devil didn't flee from them. The devil didn't flee from Paul. Paul said an angel from Satan tormented him.

The devil as the serpent in the garden is not to be taken literally. The devil didn't change into a serpent, it's a symbol of the devil. To refer to the devil as the great red dragon is to refer to the devil using a symbol just like Jesus wasn't a four legged actual lamb, it's a symbol. Jesus was the Passover Lamb. I believe the devil and his angels are manically depressed because they know that they will be cast into the lake of fire and are the cause of many people being depressed.

Years ago, I was in Beaucejour, Manitoba, it was at a water filled sand pit. I was walking along the sand with Ed Mckenna. I pointed to the water and said, "It's a lake of fire". I realized what I said was beyond my control and was scared. In the book of Enoch, there's a prophecy that a body of water will be changed to fire and that it will be God's final judgment. I don't know if it will be the lake of fire, all I know is that what I said was beyond my control. The book of Revelation says that the false prophet, the antichrist and those that received the mark of the beast will be cast into the lake of fire. Hades also known as hell is a temporary place of torment. In Revelation, it's stated that those in hell will taken out and go to the white throne judgment to be condemned and hades shall be cast into the lake of fire with those whose name are not written in the book of life.

What is meant in Ephesians 2:6, and made us sit with him in the heavenly places in Christ Jesus. I learned from Dr.Scott that when Jesus sat down in heaven it meant completed work. This means that God and Jesus views us as finished products in heaven's view even though we live on the earth.

I don't think there's person known as the Holy Spirit. Jesus used the word paraclete to describe the Holy Spirit in us as part of the trinity. Jesus started to send the paraclete at Pentecost. The saints in Christ Jesus are part of the trinity. We are the sons and daughters of the two Gods, it makes sense that we're part of the trinity.

Honey was not to be placed on the altar with offerings. I learned from Dr.Scott that honey symbolized lovy dovy mushy Christianity. I learned from Dr.Scott that agapao translated as love was to do something for someone without any expectancy of something done in return. Ezekiel's scroll that he ate tasted like honey. The scroll John eats in Revelation 10:10 tasted like honey. Honey Christians don't give offerings to preachers.

I'll mention this again. God said that if they broke the old testament covenant, he would punish them 7 times. In Daniel, time is one year, times is two years and the dividing of time is half a year. Jesus statement to Peter of forgiving 490 times wasn't about forgiving sins. It was about revealing knowledge. Daniel's seventy weeks is 490 years which is when Jesus returns as KING of kings.

Jesus' prayer in John 17 was that of the kinsman redeemer. Part of his prayer was, "that they be one, even as we are one". To be one with God and Jesus just boggles my mind. In the condition to qualify as kinsman redeemer, the kinsman had to have the price and actually had to pay it. God had said, there's no forgiveness of sins without the shedding of blood. That's why Jesus' side was pierced. The redemption price was Jesus' shed blood.

John 21:17 is written as follows: He said to him the third time, "Simon, son of John, do you love me?" Peter was grieved because he said to him the third time, "Do you love me?" In the King James version there appears to be no error but there's an error using the Greek. Jesus used the word agapao twice which is translated love and the word phileo once translated love. Therefore, John made a mistake in saying he asked three times using the same word love. In the King James Version Jesus used the word love three times but the King James Version is not accurate which is not surprising. Jesus asked him twice if he loved him and then asked him if he liked him. I learned from Dr.Scott that Jesus used the word agapao twice and the word phileo once.

I'll mention a date that I remember from Dr.Scott's teaching on the pyramid from Adam Rutherford's Book. If a line is drawn where It's October 31,1517 on the ceiling at the bottom of the descending passage and a parallel line is drawn to the bottom of the descending passage, the date is 1440 A.D. which is the date that the printing press is invented and the Gutenberg Bible is printed. This brought the church and the world out of the dark ages. It's still the greatest invention.

In Malachi, God said he loved Jacob and hated Esau. A prophecy of Jesus is that he would rule over the house of Jacob forever. Jacob was a tither and Esau wasn't.

In Ezekiel 17:22 the words, "twigs a tender one". Twigs refers to King Zedekiah's daughters. I learned from Dr.Scott that tender is feminine and referred to one of Zedekiah's daughters. Zedekiah's daughter is named Tea Tephi, she's in the lineage of successive monarchs up to Queen Elizabeth II. In Ezekiel 17:23, "In the mountain of the height of Israel will I plant it." This refers to Jeremiah taken with him Zedekiah's daughter Tea Tephi to Ireland. I remember Dr.Scott teaching that there were four prophecies about Jeremiah and that Jeremiah disappears from the Bible after two fulfilled prophecies. Jeremiah was a prophet to both houses. Dr.Scott taught that Jeremiah pulled down and destroyed five kingdoms which two fulfilled prophecies. Dr.Scott taught that the prophecies of Jeremiah planting and building the kingdom of Israel happened in Ireland. Dr.Scott taught that the King of Babylon killed all of Zedekiah's son thinking he would end the lineage of Judah because in the Babylon laws only males could be monarchs. Dr.Scott taught that in God's law, when there are no male heirs, the daughter gets the birthright.

In Hebrews 9:3, Paul used the words Holy of Holies. What does holy mean and what does holies mean? The Greek words are hagia and hagiwv. Both are from hagios. Hagios means saint and the other word is genitive plural which means of saints. What's said is: saint of saints. Jesus as High Priest was the saint of saints. I learned from Dr.Scott that being a saint had to do with commitment to God and Jesus. It had nothing to do with works of the law. I learned from Dr.Scott that the offerings placed on the altar was sainting the animal to God. The old testament animal sacrifices were types of Jesus Christ. The Holy Spirit is actually the Saintly Spirit.

What about Jesus' new law that was curse, " If you hate in your heart, you're as guilty as a murderer". It made everybody a sinner in need of God's mercy.

I consider myself a domata, to be precise, an evangelist.

Only a pyramid has a head cornerstone, its apex. Jesus Christ as the head cornerstone is in Mark 12:10. Two stars intersect in the descending passage of the pyramid, it's 2141 B.C. spring equinox, from there, one pyramid inch to a year scale, certain dates come out at junctions in the masonry. I learned from Dr.Scott's teaching on the pyramid that Jesus was born September 29, 2 B.C. The coffer in the pyramid is the same size as the ark of the covenant which symbolized God's presence. The 144,000 casing stones the pyramid had symbolizes the 144,000 sons of Israel in Revelation which is a prophecy yet to come. Dr.Scott taught that there are 203 offerings associated with the feast of tabernacles. The pyramid has 203 courses of masonry. The roof of the grand gallery which starts at the resurrection is 153 sacred cubits. The 153 fish is a parable of the church. Peter spoke in tongues at Pentecost and they heard in 17 different languages. Dr.Scott taught that if you add 1 through 17 it equals 153. The 7 tiers that opens up the grand gallery at the resurrection in the pyramid symbolizes the 7 churches in Revelation, how can the 7 churches be preached to at the same time? Because part of Revelation 2:7 is repeated 6 other times in Revelation which means what's said to one church is said to all 7 churches at the same time. The Holy of Holies in the tabernacle and Solomon's temple is 20 x 20 sacred cubits which is the size of the upper chamber in the pyramid. The pyramid is prophesied in Isaiah 19:19. The letters of the Hebrew alphabet have a numerical value. The numerical value of Isaiah 19:19 in Hebrew is 5,449 and the height of the pyramid is 5,449

Ray

pyramid inches which is not an accident. The Christ triangle in the pyramid, if placed on the north face of the pyramid and its hypotenuse extended hits Bethlehem which is not an accident. Dr.Scott taught that the stones blown upward in the lower chamber symbolized the power of the resurrection. The bottom of the descending passage is October 31, 1517, the start of the Sardis church which is when Martin Luther nailed his 95 thesis to the door of Wittenberg. The end of the roof of the grand gallery, the date is the start of World War I and ends the Sardis church. The junction of the ascending and descending passages, the date is 1453 B.C., which is Passover, the exodus out of Egypt. Dr.Scott taught that if a line is drawn from the south east corner of the pyramid to the north west corner and extended over the earth it will hit Stonehenge. Dr.Scott taught that 6 is the number of a man in the prophecy of buying a Hebrew slave. Adam was created on the 6th day. The pyramid is not a pyramid yet because it has 6 sides and speaks of Jesus Christ's control over history. Before the flood, a religion of Enoch was God's message in the stars. Dr.Scott taught on the mystery of the sphinx, it's head is Virgo and back half of a lion which is Leo. He said, start with Virgo and end with Leo. Virgo was the virgin Mary and the lion was the lion of the tribe of Judah Jesus Christ. Dr.Scott taught on the great step in the pyramid was Daniel's prophesy that knowledge would be increased. The date of the great step is 1845, which is when scholars went down to Egypt and made discoveries and when the book of Enoch was rediscovered. Dr.Scott taught that the passage way is 286.1 inches to the left and the coffer is 286.1 inches to the right and if a capstone was placed on the pyramid built from the four socket stones, the bottom of the capstone would overlap the existing pyramid by 8 x 286.1 pyramid inches which is not an accident.